This Text Book is useful for Savitribai Phule Pune University and other Universities of Maharashtra as well as Competitive Exams.

ADVANCED BANKING & FINANCE

(Universal Banking)

(MM) (Course Code : 60122)

M.Com (Sem. - I)

As per New Education Policy (2020)

Dr. Kishor S. Nikam
(M.Com., NET., SET., Ph.D., CA Final (II)., DTL., GDC&A., MBA., DMB., PGDBM., ADM., MA., DLL & LW., DIPR., DCCL)
Dr. D. Y. Patil ACS College, Pimpri, Pune.

Dr. Sonali M. Chindhade
(M.Com., M. Phil., Ph.D.)
B.Y.K. College of Commerce

Dr. Vijay D. Nirmal
(M.Com., M. Phil., SET., Ph.D.)
Padmashri Vikhe Patil College of ACS., Pravaranagar.

Dr. Vinit Rakibe
(M.Com., M.Phil., NET., SET., MBA., Ph.D.)
Loknete Vyankatrao Hiray College., Nashik.

2023

Price: 55/-

SUCCESS PUBLICATIONS

AF517219

Published by
Dr. Rajesh M. Patne
Success Publications
Radha Krishna Apartment, 535, Shaniwar Peth,
Appa Balwant Chowk, Opp. Prabhat Talkies, Pune - 411 030.
Ph. 24434662 Mobile : 9325315464.

Edition
2023

Edited By
Mr. Valmik Gaikwad

Typesetting, Layout
Miss. Akanksha Pingle

Cover Designing
Miss. Varsha Lokhande

ISBN NO. – 978-81-19180-51-6

Preface

It is a matter of great pleasure for us to present this book to our esteemed readers. This book has been designed as standard text on 'Advanced Banking & Finance (Universal Banking (Course Code 60122)' for M.Com. (Sem. - I).

This book comprehensively covers the entire syllabus of M.Com. (Advanced Banking & Finance (Universal Banking (Course Code 60122) Course of Savitribai Phule Pune University effective from 2023 onwards. It has been written to meet the requirements of students of M.Com. Some of the special features of the book are as follows:

1. *Full coverage of the revised syllabus of M.Com.*
2. *Chapter outline at the beginning of each chapter to give a bird's eye view of the topics covered in the chapter.*
3. *Point wise explanation of each topic in the chapter.*
4. *Topics are logically arranged in numbered paragraphs exactly according to the modified syllabus.*
5. *Proposed questions at the end of each chapter.*
6. *Extensive use of diagrams, tables and various forms to give visual view of key concepts and techniques.*
7. *Conversational, lucid and simple language.*

Every effort has been made to provide the readers with most up-to-date and authentic material on the subject.

We are very grateful to our publisher Mrs. and Mr. Rajesh Patne who have rendered all possible assistance in bringing out this book. We wish to acknowledge our deep gratitude to staff who have assisted and helped us in preparing this book. We will consider our efforts amply rewarded in case the book proves useful to the students and teachers of the subject.

Suggestions of readers are welcome and shall be acknowledged with gratitude.

With best wishes.

By Authors

Syllabus

M.Com.- I (Sem. - I) Advanced Banking & Finance
Universal Banking (MM) (Course Code : 60122)

Unit No.	Title with Contents	No. of Lectures
I	**Evolution of Universal Banking in India**	**15**
	i. Evolution of Universal Banking in India Meaning, Definition, Objective, Characteristics of Universal Banking **ii.** Difference between Commercial Banking and Universal Banking Functions of Universal Banks	
II	**Practices of Universal Banks**	**15**
	i. Practices of Universal Banks **ii.** Advantages and Disadvantages of Universal Banking **iii.** Problems Faced by the Universal Banks **iv.** Recent Trends in Universal Banking in India	

INDEX

M.Com.- I (Sem. - I) Advanced Banking & Finance
Universal Banking (MM) (Course Code : 60122)

UNIT 1

Evolution of Universal Banking System in India

Introduction :

The evolution of the Universal Banking System in India has been a significant journey marked by progressive liberalization and regulatory reforms. Before 1991, the banking sector was dominated by public sector banks with limited offerings. The economic reforms in 1991 opened the doors for private and foreign banks, allowing them to provide a broader range of financial services. The introduction of new private sector banks in the 1990s further contributed to the concept of universal banking gaining traction. Over the years, there has been a focus on financial inclusion and technology integration, enabling banks to offer digital services. As a result, the Indian banking landscape has transformed, offering customers a comprehensive suite of banking, investment, insurance, and digital services under one roof.

1.1 Universal Banking System in India:

Universal Banking System refers to a banking model where financial institutions offer a complete range of financial services under one umbrella, including commercial banking, investment banking, insurance, asset management, and other related services. Unlike traditional banking models, universal banks can engage in multiple financial activities, catering to the diverse needs of both individual and corporate clients. This integrated approach allows for cross-selling of products, enhanced customer convenience, and risk diversification for the bank. While universal banking offers potential benefits in terms of efficiency and financial stability, it also raises concerns about potential conflicts of interest and systemic risks. Regulatory oversight and prudent risk management are essential to maintain the stability and integrity of universal banking operations.

1.1.1 Meaning:

Universal Banking refers to a comprehensive financial services model where a single institution offers a wide range of banking and financial products and services, including commercial banking, investment banking, insurance, asset management, and other related activities. This integrated approach allows customers to access a diverse array of financial offerings under one roof, simplifying their banking experience and fostering cross-selling opportunities for the institution. Universal banks can cater to the needs of individuals, businesses, and corporations across various financial sectors, promoting efficiency, convenience, and potential economies of scale. However, the concept also raises concerns about potential conflicts of interest and systemic risks, necessitating effective regulatory oversight and risk management to maintain the stability and integrity of such institutions.

1.1.2 Definitions:

The following are the definitions of Universal Banking System:

1) **Dr. G. R. Bhatia:**

   "Universal Banking refers to a banking system where financial institutions offer a complete range of financial services, including commercial banking, investment banking, and insurance, thus providing a one-stop-shop for all banking and financial needs."

2) **Dr. Alok Kumar Mishra**:

   "a system where banks are allowed to offer a diverse set of financial services, encompassing commercial, investment, and merchant banking, insurance, and other allied activities, promoting financial inclusion and convenience for customers."

3) **Jan Pieter Krahnen and Reinhard H. Schmidt:**

   "A financial intermediation model where banks combine various financial services under one entity, breaking the traditional boundaries between banking and non-banking activities, to maximize synergies and offer a holistic range of services to clients."

1.1.3 Evolution of Universal Banking System in India:

The evolution of the Universal Banking System in India has been a transformative journey marked by regulatory reforms, economic liberalization, and technological advancements. This comprehensive financial model, which offers a wide array of financial services under one roof, has significantly altered the landscape of the Indian banking sector and contributed to the country's economic growth.

A) **Pre-Liberalization Era:**

   Prior to economic liberalization in the early 1990s, India's banking sector was characterized by a highly regulated environment with limited competition and strict segmentation between different financial services. Commercial banks were primarily focused on traditional banking activities, while other financial services were offered by separate institutions, such as development financial institutions and non-banking financial companies (NBFCs).

B) Economic Liberalization and Regulatory Reforms:

The initiation of economic liberalization in 1991 marked a turning point for the Indian economy and its banking sector. The government introduced reforms to open up the financial sector, attract foreign investment, and encourage competition. Key regulatory changes that facilitated the evolution of universal banking in India include:

1) Banking Sector Reforms (1991-1997):

The Narasimham Committee's recommendations led to reforms in the banking sector, including measures to enhance transparency, strengthen prudential norms, and encourage the adoption of international best practices. These reforms laid the foundation for a more robust and diversified banking system.

2) Entry of New Banks and Licensing Policies:

The Reserve Bank of India (RBI) began to grant licenses to new private sector banks and foreign banks, increasing competition and diversifying the range of services offered in the banking sector.

3) Branch Licensing and Financial Inclusion:

The RBI adopted a more liberal approach to branch licensing, enabling banks to expand their networks. This facilitated increased outreach to unbanked and underbanked areas, contributing to financial inclusion efforts.

C) Emergence of Universal Banks:

The late 1990s and early 2000s witnessed the emergence of universal banks in India, offering a comprehensive range of financial services under a single umbrella. Several factors contributed to this transformation:

1) Regulatory Framework for Universal Banks:

The RBI introduced the concept of "universal banking" by allowing banks to diversify into various financial services, including investment banking, insurance, and asset management, subject to regulatory approvals.

2) Entry of Foreign Banks:

The entry of foreign banks with global expertise in universal banking practices further influenced the evolution of Indian banks towards a more diversified service model.

3) Technological Advancements:

The adoption of technology, including the expansion of electronic banking and the Internet, facilitated the offering of a broader range of services and enhanced customer experience.

D) Post-Global Financial Crisis and Technological Integration:

The global financial crisis of 2008 prompted a renewed focus on risk management, regulatory compliance, and corporate governance in the banking sector. This period also witnessed significant technological integration, as banks embraced digital platforms, online banking, and mobile banking services to cater to evolving customer preferences.

E) Recent Developments:

In recent years, the evolution of universal banking in India has continued to progress in response to dynamic market conditions and changing consumer expectations:

1) Fintech Integration:

Indian banks are increasingly collaborating with fintech companies to offer innovative financial products and services, ranging from digital wallets to robo-advisory services.

2) Digital Transformation:

The "Digital India" initiative has accelerated the digital transformation of the banking sector, enabling universal banks to provide customers with seamless online experiences and real-time services.

3) Expansion of Services:

Universal banks in India are expanding their service offerings to include wealth management, advisory services, and customized financial solutions for individuals and businesses.

4) Risk Management and Corporate Governance:

Regulatory emphasis on risk management, corporate governance, and financial stability continues to shape the practices and strategies of universal banks.

5) Financial Inclusion:

Universal banks are contributing to financial inclusion efforts by leveraging technology to extend banking services to previously underserved segments of the population.

1.1.4 Objectives of Universal Banking:

The objectives of the Universal Banking System are multifaceted and encompass various aspects of the financial sector. Some of the primary objectives include:

1) Comprehensive Financial Services:

The main objective of universal banking is to offer a wide range of financial services under one roof. By providing services such as commercial banking, investment banking, insurance, asset management, and other related activities, universal banks aim to cater to the diverse financial needs of individuals, businesses, and corporations.

2) **Convenience for Customers:**
Universal banking seeks to enhance customer convenience by allowing them to access various financial products and services from a single institution. This integrated approach simplifies banking for customers and reduces the need to deal with multiple financial entities.

3) **Cross-Selling Opportunities:**
Universal banks can leverage cross-selling opportunities by offering a comprehensive suite of financial products. For example, a bank can offer investment products to its commercial banking clients or insurance products to its retail customers, thereby maximizing revenue generation.

4) **Risk Diversification:**
By engaging in multiple financial activities, universal banks can spread their risks across different sectors and geographies. This diversification helps in reducing the impact of adverse events in one area on the overall financial stability of the institution.

5) **Economies of Scale:**
Universal banking allows banks to benefit from economies of scale by consolidating various services and operations. This can lead to cost efficiencies and improved profitability for the institution.

6) **Enhanced Financial Inclusion:**
Universal banks can play a crucial role in promoting financial inclusion by reaching out to a broader segment of the population with a diverse range of financial services, including those in rural and underserved areas.

7) **Increased Competition and Innovation:**
The presence of universal banks in the financial market enhances competition and innovation. These institutions often introduce new and innovative products and services to meet the evolving needs of customers and compete with specialized financial entities.

8) **Support for Economic Growth:**
Universal banking systems can facilitate economic growth by providing a more efficient and diversified financial intermediation process. This, in turn, can aid in the allocation of capital to productive sectors and support overall economic development.

1.1.5 Characteristics of Universal Banking:

Universal Banking is a comprehensive financial services model where a single institution offers a wide range of banking and financial products and services under one roof. The concept of universal banking has evolved over time, and its characteristics have been shaped by economic, regulatory, and market developments.

1) Diverse Range of Services:

The primary characteristic of universal banking is the diverse range of financial services offered by a single institution. Universal banks engage in traditional commercial banking activities, such as accepting deposits and providing loans to individuals and businesses. Additionally, they provide investment banking services, including underwriting securities, facilitating mergers and acquisitions, and advising on capital raising activities. Moreover, universal banks offer insurance products and asset management services to cater to various financial needs of their customers.

2) Integration of Activities:

Universal banking breaks down the traditional barriers between different financial activities. In a universal banking model, various financial services are integrated, allowing customers to access multiple products and services from a single source. This integration fosters cross-selling opportunities, where banks can offer different products to their existing customers, maximizing revenue generation and customer retention.

3) Risk Diversification:

One of the advantages of universal banking is the ability to spread risks across various financial activities. By engaging in multiple sectors, universal banks can diversify their revenue streams and reduce exposure to adverse events in any single sector. For example, during economic downturns, investment banking activities might face challenges, but the stability of commercial banking and insurance operations can help offset potential losses.

4) Economies of Scale:

Universal banks can benefit from economies of scale by consolidating various financial activities under one entity. This consolidation allows for cost efficiencies and improved profitability as shared resources and infrastructures are used across different business lines. Economies of scale can be particularly beneficial in enhancing the competitiveness of universal banks compared to specialized financial institutions.

5) Customer Convenience:

The integration of services in universal banking results in enhanced customer convenience. Customers can access a wide range of financial products and services through a single banking relationship, reducing the need to deal with multiple financial institutions. This convenience fosters customer loyalty and satisfaction.

6) Enhanced Financial Inclusion:

Universal banks can play a pivotal role in promoting financial inclusion by reaching out to a broader segment of the population with diverse financial services. Through their extensive branch networks and digital platforms, universal banks can extend their services to rural and underserved areas, offering access to financial products that were previously unavailable to many individuals and businesses.

7) Cross-Border Operations:

Universal banks are often multinational in nature, with operations spread across different countries and regions. This global presence enables them to serve multinational corporations and international clients, facilitating cross-border financial transactions and investments.

8) Regulatory Challenges:

The universal banking model poses unique regulatory challenges due to the integration of various financial activities. Regulators need to strike a balance between promoting financial stability and innovation while addressing potential conflicts of interest and systemic risks. Effective regulatory oversight is essential to maintain the integrity and stability of universal banking institutions.

9) Potential Conflicts of Interest:

Universal banks' diverse activities may lead to potential conflicts of interest between different business lines. For example, an investment banking arm might recommend products or services from the commercial banking division, which could raise concerns about impartiality and consumer protection. Managing these conflicts requires robust internal controls and compliance mechanisms.

10) Systemic Risk:

The interconnectedness of universal banks with various financial activities can contribute to systemic risk. The failure of a universal bank could have far-reaching implications for the financial system, affecting multiple sectors and economies. As a result, regulators need to carefully monitor and assess the systemic importance of universal banks and implement appropriate risk management measures.

11) Financial Stability and Resilience:

The ability of universal banks to withstand financial shocks and maintain stability is a critical aspect of their operations. Risk management practices, stress testing, and capital adequacy requirements are essential elements in ensuring the resilience of universal banking institutions.

12) Innovation and Competition:

The presence of universal banks in the financial market enhances competition and fosters innovation. These institutions often introduce new and innovative products and services to meet the evolving needs of customers and compete with specialized financial entities.

13) Impact on Banking Landscape:

Universal banking has significantly impacted the banking landscape. While traditional banks still exist, the presence of universal banks has challenged the dominance of specialized institutions. Customers' preferences for comprehensive financial services have led to a shift in the competitive dynamics of the banking sector.

14) Corporate Governance:

The complexity of universal banking operations necessitates robust corporate governance practices to ensure effective oversight and risk management. Strong corporate governance frameworks are essential in safeguarding the interests of shareholders, customers, and other stakeholders.

15) Market Concentration:

The expansion of universal banks can lead to increased market concentration, which might raise concerns about competition and consumer choice. Regulators need to monitor market dynamics to prevent potential anti-competitive practices.

1.1.6 Importance of Universal Banking:

Universal banking is a comprehensive financial model in which financial institutions offer a wide range of banking and financial services to customers under a single roof. This model contrasts with specialized banking, where institutions focus on specific financial activities. Universal banking's significance stems from its potential to enhance financial stability, customer convenience, efficiency, and economic growth.

1) **Financial Stability and Risk Diversification:**

   Universal banks are equipped to diversify their revenue streams across various financial activities, including retail banking, investment banking, asset management, and insurance. This diversification reduces the institution's reliance on a single revenue source and minimizes exposure to volatility in specific sectors. During economic downturns, this risk diversification can contribute to overall financial stability by mitigating the impact of losses in one area with gains from others.

2) **Customer Convenience and One-Stop Services:**

   Universal banking simplifies customers' financial interactions by providing a comprehensive range of services under one roof. Customers can manage their savings, investments, loans, insurance, and more through a single institution, streamlining their financial activities and reducing the need to engage with multiple providers. This convenience enhances the customer experience and encourages loyalty.

3) **Efficient Resource Allocation:**

   Under the universal banking model, institutions can optimize the allocation of their resources by deploying capital and personnel across different banking segments based on market conditions and demand. This flexibility enables banks to adapt to changing economic environments and maximize their operational efficiency.

4) **Cross-Selling Opportunities:**

   Universal banks can leverage their broad range of services to cross-sell products and services to their existing customer base. For example, a bank's retail customers might also be interested in investment opportunities, insurance products, or mortgage services offered by the same institution. This cross-selling strategy enhances revenue generation and customer retention.

5) **Access to Funding and Capital Markets:**
Universal banks can tap into diverse funding sources and capital markets due to their multifunctional nature. This access to various funding channels ensures that banks can raise capital and funds more efficiently, enabling them to support lending activities and fuel economic growth.

6) **Facilitating Economic Growth:**
By offering a comprehensive suite of financial services, universal banks play a pivotal role in promoting economic growth. They support businesses by providing credit, investment, and capital market services. Additionally, their role in retail banking contributes to individual consumers' access to credit and financial products, which stimulates consumption and economic activity.

7) **Economies of Scale:**
Universal banks can benefit from economies of scale by sharing infrastructure, resources, and technology across different business segments. This synergy leads to cost savings that can be passed on to customers through competitive pricing and improved services.

8) **Innovation and Technological Advancements:**
The universal banking model encourages innovation and technological advancements. Financial institutions that offer a wide range of services are more likely to invest in advanced technology, digital platforms, and fintech collaborations to enhance their offerings and stay competitive in a rapidly evolving financial landscape.

9) **Internationalization and Global Operations:**
Universal banks are well-positioned to expand their operations across borders, offering their suite of financial services in multiple countries. This internationalization enhances their reach, diversifies their client base, and contributes to the global flow of capital and investments.

10) **Regulatory Framework and Risk Management:**
Universal banks are often subject to comprehensive regulatory frameworks due to the complexities of their operations. This scrutiny promotes transparency, accountability, and adherence to risk management practices, thereby reducing the likelihood of financial crises and systemic risks.

11) **Integrated Financial Services:**
Universal banks can offer integrated financial solutions that cater to the evolving needs of customers. For instance, they can create tailor-made solutions that combine banking, insurance, and investment products to address specific financial goals.

12) Wealth Management and Financial Advisory:

The universal banking model allows for the integration of wealth management and financial advisory services. Customers can receive holistic advice that considers their entire financial situation, resulting in better-informed decisions.

1.2 Difference Between Universal Banking & Commercial Banking:

Universal Banking and Commercial Banking are two distinct financial services models with different characteristics, objectives, and scope of operations.

1) **Range of Services:**

   One of the primary differences between Universal Banking and Commercial Banking lies in the range of services they offer. Commercial banks primarily focus on traditional banking activities, such as accepting deposits, providing loans, and offering basic financial products to individuals and businesses. On the other hand, Universal Banks go beyond traditional banking and offer a diverse range of financial services, including commercial banking, investment banking, insurance, asset management, and other related activities. The integration of multiple financial services distinguishes Universal Banking from the more limited scope of Commercial Banking.

2) **Integration of Activities:**

   Commercial banking typically operates as a stand-alone entity, offering banking services exclusively. Commercial banks do not engage in non-banking activities like investment banking or insurance. In contrast, Universal Banks integrate various financial activities under one roof, breaking down the traditional barriers between banking and non-banking activities. This integration allows Universal Banks to cross-sell products and offer comprehensive financial solutions to their customers.

3) **Risk Diversification:**

   Risk diversification is another significant difference between Universal Banking and Commercial Banking. Commercial banks usually focus on traditional banking activities, and their risk exposure is primarily related to lending and deposit-taking activities. In contrast, Universal Banks engage in multiple financial sectors, including investment banking, asset management, and insurance. As a result, Universal Banks can spread their risks across different areas, reducing their exposure to adverse events in any single sector.

4) **Regulatory Environment:**

   The regulatory environment for Universal Banking and Commercial Banking differs due to their distinct business models and risk profiles. Commercial banks are subject to regulations that focus on prudential norms, capital adequacy, liquidity requirements, and deposit protection. The regulatory framework for Commercial Banking is primarily centered around traditional banking risks and stability. On the other hand, Universal Banks face more complex and comprehensive regulations due to their involvement in diverse financial activities. Regulators must address potential conflicts of interest, systemic risk, and ensure adequate risk management across all business lines.

5) **Customer Focus:**

While both Universal Banking and Commercial Banking serve customers, their customer focus differs to some extent. Commercial banks primarily cater to the banking needs of individuals, small and medium-sized enterprises (SMEs), and corporate clients. They offer standard banking products like savings accounts, checking accounts, and loans. Universal Banks, on the other hand, target a broader customer base, ranging from individuals and SMEs to large corporations and institutional clients. Their integrated services provide customers with a more comprehensive suite of financial solutions.

6) **Financial Inclusion:**

Financial inclusion is a key aspect that sets Universal Banking apart from Commercial Banking. Universal Banks, with their diverse range of services and extensive branch networks, have the potential to play a more significant role in promoting financial inclusion. They can reach out to rural and underserved areas, offering a broader set of financial products and services to a more diverse segment of the population.

7) **Impact on the Financial Sector:**

The presence of Universal Banks and Commercial Banks has a distinct impact on the financial sector. Universal Banks, with their integrated approach, challenge the dominance of specialized financial institutions. They promote competition and innovation by offering a wide range of financial products and services. Commercial Banks, while serving as the backbone of traditional banking services, compete based on their efficiency, customer service, and localized presence.

8) **Size and Complexity:**

Universal Banks are typically larger and more complex institutions compared to Commercial Banks. The integration of various financial activities requires a sophisticated organizational structure, expertise across multiple domains, and a more extensive network of branches and subsidiaries. Commercial Banks, while also operating on a large scale, do not face the same level of complexity in their operations.

9) **Risk Management Practices:**

Due to their diverse activities, Universal Banks have more complex risk management practices compared to Commercial Banks. Universal Banks must implement robust risk management frameworks to address the potential risks associated with different financial sectors. They need to manage credit risk, market risk, operational risk, and other types of risk across their diverse operations.

10) Cross-Border Operations:

Universal Banks are often multinational in nature, with operations spread across different countries and regions. They can serve multinational corporations and international clients, facilitating cross-border financial transactions and investments. Commercial Banks, while they may have international operations, typically have a more localized focus.

Here's a comparison between Universal Banking and Commercial Banking in a table format:

Aspect	Universal Banking	Commercial Banking
Range of Services	Offers a wide range of financial services, including retail banking, investment banking, asset management, insurance, and more.	Primarily focuses on traditional banking services such as accepting deposits, providing loans, and facilitating basic financial transactions.
Scope	Provides comprehensive financial solutions under one roof, catering to various financial needs of customers.	Primarily focuses on core banking services without the extensive diversification seen in universal banking.
Risk Diversification	Diversifies risks across multiple sectors and services, as losses in one segment can be offset by gains in others.	Limited risk diversification, as commercial banks primarily rely on traditional banking activities.
Customer Convenience	Offers a one-stop-shop for customers, allowing them to access various financial services without the need for multiple institutions.	Offers basic banking services without the convenience of a comprehensive suite of offerings.
Cross-Selling	Capitalizes on cross-selling opportunities by offering additional products and services to existing customers.	May engage in cross-selling to a lesser extent, usually focusing on core banking products.
International Presence	Often has an international presence, offering services across borders and catering to global clients.	Primarily operates within the local market, with limited international operations.
Regulatory Framework	Subject to comprehensive regulatory oversight due to the	Subject to regulatory frameworks that pertain to basic banking

Aspect	Universal Banking	Commercial Banking
	complexity of services offered.	activities.
Technological Innovation	Often invests in advanced technology, digital platforms, and fintech collaborations to enhance customer experience and competitiveness.	May invest in technology but with a narrower focus compared to universal banks.
Economic Impact	Plays a significant role in promoting economic growth by supporting businesses and individual consumers with diverse financial services.	Contributes to economic growth by providing essential banking services to individuals and businesses.
Revenue Streams	Generates revenue from a wide range of financial activities, including fee-based services, investment banking, and insurance.	Generates revenue mainly from interest income on loans and interest paid on deposits.

1.3 Functions of Universal Banks:

Universal banks, also known as full-service banks or financial conglomerates, perform a wide range of functions that go beyond traditional commercial banking activities. Their comprehensive business model enables them to offer diverse financial services, including commercial banking, investment banking, insurance, asset management, and other related activities.

1) **Commercial Banking Functions:**
   At the core of universal banks' functions are traditional commercial banking activities. These functions include accepting deposits from individuals and businesses, providing various types of loans (personal loans, home loans, business loans, etc.), offering checking and savings accounts, and facilitating electronic fund transfers. Universal banks play a vital role in intermediating funds between savers and borrowers, providing liquidity to the economy, and supporting financial inclusion.

2) **Investment Banking Functions:**
   Universal banks have a strong presence in investment banking activities, serving as intermediaries in capital markets. They underwrite and distribute securities, such as stocks and bonds, assisting corporations and governments in raising capital through initial public offerings (IPOs) and bond issuances. Investment banking functions also include providing financial advisory services on mergers and acquisitions (M&A), restructuring, and corporate finance.

3) **Wealth Management and Asset Management:**

Universal banks offer wealth management services to high-net-worth individuals and institutional clients. These services include personalized financial planning, portfolio management, estate planning, and tax advisory. Additionally, universal banks operate asset management divisions that manage various investment funds, including mutual funds, exchange-traded funds (ETFs), and other investment products.

4) **Insurance Services:**

Universal banks often have insurance subsidiaries or divisions that offer a range of insurance products to individuals and businesses. These products include life insurance, health insurance, property insurance, and casualty insurance. By providing insurance services, universal banks can diversify their revenue streams and offer comprehensive financial solutions to their clients.

5) **Treasury and Forex Operations:**

Universal banks manage their own treasury operations, which involve investing excess funds in various financial instruments to maximize returns. They also engage in foreign exchange (forex) operations to facilitate international trade and manage currency risks for their clients.

6) **Retail Banking Services:**

As part of their commercial banking functions, universal banks offer a wide range of retail banking services to individual customers. These services include ATM facilities, debit and credit card issuance, online and mobile banking, and customer support for various banking needs.

7) **Corporate Banking and Trade Finance:**

Universal banks provide corporate banking services to businesses and corporations. These services include working capital financing, trade finance, cash management solutions, and corporate advisory. Trade finance facilitates international trade by providing letters of credit, export financing, and trade-related services.

8) **Project Finance and Infrastructure Funding:**

Universal banks often participate in project finance, providing long-term financing for infrastructure projects, energy ventures, and other large-scale initiatives. They structure the financing and assess the risks associated with these projects to attract investors and lenders.

9) **Capital Market Services:**

Universal banks offer a broad range of capital market services, including equity research, equity brokerage, and fixed-income trading. They act as intermediaries in secondary market transactions, facilitating the buying and selling of securities for their clients.

10) **Financial Advisory and Investment Services:**

Universal banks provide financial advisory services to clients, assisting them in making informed decisions about their investments, financial planning, and wealth management. These advisory services help clients achieve their financial goals and optimize their investment strategies.

11) **Electronic and Digital Banking:**

Universal banks invest heavily in technology and offer electronic and digital banking services. This includes online banking, mobile banking applications, and digital wallets, enabling customers to conduct transactions, access account information, and make payments conveniently.

12) **Real Estate and Mortgage Services:**

Some universal banks have specialized real estate divisions that provide financing and advisory services for real estate projects. They offer mortgage loans to individuals for home purchases, further diversifying their lending portfolio.

13) **Private Equity and Venture Capital:**

Universal banks may have private equity and venture capital arms that invest in start-ups, growing businesses, and innovative ventures. These investments support entrepreneurial endeavors and foster innovation in various industries.

14) **Cross-Border Services:**

Universal banks with a global presence facilitate cross-border banking services, enabling international trade and investments. They offer correspondent banking services, trade finance, foreign exchange, and international fund transfers to support cross-border transactions.

15) **Financial Inclusion Initiatives:**

Universal banks play a crucial role in promoting financial inclusion, especially in emerging economies. They extend their services to underserved areas, offering basic banking facilities to unbanked populations and supporting microfinance initiatives.

16) **Risk Management and Compliance:**

Universal banks have dedicated risk management and compliance functions to identify, assess, and manage various risks associated with their diverse operations. They comply with regulatory requirements, anti-money laundering (AML) regulations, and data security protocols to safeguard their clients and maintain the integrity of the financial system.

17) **Research and Market Insights:**

Universal banks conduct market research and provide insights into economic trends, investment opportunities, and financial market developments. Their research reports and analysis help clients make informed financial decisions.

18) Corporate Social Responsibility (CSR):

Many universal banks actively engage in CSR initiatives, supporting community development, education, healthcare, and environmental sustainability. They contribute to social welfare and address the needs of the communities they serve.

****

Multiple Choice Questions

1) _______________ is a banking model where financial institutions provide a wide range of banking and financial services under a single roof.

a) Financial management
b) Universal Banking
c) Cultural integration
d) Linguistic diversity

2) The concept of universal banking gained prominence in India after _______________ introduced financial sector reforms in the 1990s.

a) quality control
b) the Reserve Bank of India (RBI)
c) inventory management
d) economic liberalization

3) In a universal banking system, a single financial institution can offer services such as _______________, insurance, asset management, and investment banking.

a) Financial analysis
b) retail banking
c) supply chain management
d) linguistic diversity

4) The adoption of universal banking aims to _______________ by providing convenience and comprehensive financial solutions to customers.

a) enhance financial stability
b) cultural integration
c) linguistic diversity
d) inventory management

5) _______________ is the regulatory authority in India that oversees the banking sector and formulates guidelines for universal banking operations.

a) The Securities and Exchange Board of India (SEBI)
b) The Ministry of Finance
c) The Competition Commission of India
d) The Reserve Bank of India (RBI)

6) Universal banking in India has led to increased _______________ between banking and other financial services, benefiting both customers and financial institutions.

a) quality control
b) financial integration
c) inventory optimization
d) linguistic diversity

7) _______________ refers to a banking model where financial institutions offer a wide range of financial services beyond traditional banking activities.

a) Financial management
b) Universal Banking
c) Cultural integration
d) Linguistic diversity

8) **The ________________ of universal banking involves providing various financial services under a single corporate entity.**
   a) quality control
   b) definition
   c) inventory management
   d) artistic expressions

9) **The ________________ of universal banking is to provide convenience to customers by offering diverse financial services in one place.**
   a) Financial analysis
   b) objective
   c) supply chain management
   d) linguistic diversity

10) **One of the key ________________ of universal banking is the integration of banking, insurance, asset management, and investment banking services.**
   a) quality control
   b) characteristics
   c) financial analysis
   d) cultural integration

11) **Universal banking aims to enhance customer ________________ by providing comprehensive financial solutions and convenience.**
   a) linguistic diversity
   b) quality control
   c) satisfaction
   d) inventory management

12) **The ________________ of universal banking includes financial stability, increased cross-selling opportunities, and improved competitiveness.**
   a) cultural integration
   b) characteristics
   c) linguistic diversity
   d) objective

13) **________________ primarily involves offering core banking services like deposits, loans, and basic financial products to retail and corporate customers.**
   a) Financial management
   b) Commercial Banking
   c) Cultural integration
   d) Linguistic diversity

14) **In contrast, ________________ includes a broader range of financial services such as insurance, investment banking, and wealth management.**
   a) quality control
   b) Universal Banking
   c) inventory management
   d) artistic expressions

15) **________________ focus on traditional banking activities and do not engage extensively in non-banking financial services.**
   a) Financial analysis
   b) Commercial banks
   c) Supply chain management
   d) Linguistic diversity

16) **________________ institutions offer a one-stop-shop for various financial needs, catering to diverse customer requirements.**
   a) Commercial Banking
   b) Universal Banking
   c) Financial analysis
   d) Cultural integration

17) While commercial banks concentrate on _______________ financial services, universal banks provide an integrated suite of financial products.

a) inventory management b) core

c) linguistic diversity d) quality control

18) The key distinction lies in the _______________ range of services offered, with universal banking being a more comprehensive approach.

a) cultural integration b) linguistic diversity

c) scope and d) financial analysis

19) Universal banks offer _______________ services, such as savings accounts, fixed deposits, and loans, to individuals and businesses.

a) Financial management b) retail banking

c) Cultural integration d) Linguistic diversity

20) They also provide _______________ services like investment banking, underwriting, and trading of financial instruments.

a) quality control b) wholesale banking

c) inventory management d) artistic expressions

21) _______________ is a function of universal banks that involves helping clients manage their investment portfolios and achieve financial goals.

a) Financial analysis b) Wealth management

c) Supply chain management d) Linguistic diversity

22) Universal banks often engage in _______________ activities, offering insurance products to individuals and businesses.

a) quality control b) insurance

c) financial analysis d) cultural integration

23) They assist corporations in raising capital through _______________ activities like Initial Public Offerings (IPOs) and bond issuance.

a) inventory management b) investment banking

c) linguistic diversity d) quality control

24) Universal banks act as _______________ intermediaries by facilitating the trading of securities, foreign exchange, and derivatives.

a) cultural integration b) financial

c) linguistic diversity d) inventory management

Ans : **1)** b, **2)** d, **3)** d, **4)** a, **5)** d, **6)** b, **7)** b, **8)** b, **9)** b, **10)** b, **11)** c, **12)** d, **13)** b, **14)** b, **15)** b, **16)** b, **17)** b, **18)** c, **19)** b, **20)** b, **21)** b, **22)** b, **23)** b, **24)** b.

Review Questions

Q.1. What is Universal Banking? Discuss about the Evolution of Universal Banking System in India.

Q.2. Discuss the Objectives of Universal Banking

Q.3. Explain the Characteristics of Universal Banking.

Q.4. Discuss the Importance of Universal Banking.

Q.5. State the Difference between Commercial Banking and Universal Banking.

Q.6. Explain about the Functions of Universal Banking.

Q.7. Write the Short Notes on Following:

- **a)** Objective of Universal Banking.
- **b)** Characteristics of Universal Banking.
- **c)** Functions of Universal Banks.
- **d)** Difference between Commercial Banking and Universal Banking.

****

UNIT 2

Practices of Universal Banks

Introduction:

Practices of Universal Banks encompass a wide array of strategic and operational approaches, reflecting their integrated business model. These banks engage in comprehensive risk management practices, accounting for the diverse risks associated with their various financial activities. They emphasize cross-selling by offering tailored financial solutions to customers, leveraging their multifaceted service portfolio to deepen customer relationships. Universal Banks also prioritize technology integration, developing advanced digital platforms and mobile apps to enhance customer convenience and accessibility. Their corporate governance involves robust internal controls, risk committees, and compliance frameworks to address potential conflicts of interest and ensure ethical conduct across different business lines. Moreover, Universal Banks actively contribute to economic development through corporate social responsibility initiatives, supporting education, healthcare, and sustainable initiatives to benefit the communities they serve.

2.1 Practices of Universal Banks:

Practices of Universal Banks encompass a comprehensive array of strategic, operational, and ethical approaches that define the way these financial institutions operate within the global financial landscape. As institutions offering an extensive range of financial services, including commercial banking, investment banking, insurance, asset management, and more, universal banks engage in a variety of practices to effectively manage risks, optimize revenue, enhance customer experience, promote innovation, ensure regulatory compliance, and contribute positively to society.

1) **Integrated Risk Management:**

One of the cornerstones of universal banking practices is integrated risk management. Given their involvement in various financial activities, universal banks need to identify, assess, and manage a diverse range of risks, including credit risk, market risk, operational risk, and regulatory risk. Effective risk management practices involve developing comprehensive risk assessment models that consider the interconnectedness of different business lines. This approach ensures that risks are properly understood and mitigated across all operations, minimizing the potential impact of adverse events on the institution's stability.

2) **Cross-Selling and Synergy Creation:**

Universal banks capitalize on their diverse service offerings by practicing cross-selling, a strategy where they offer multiple financial products and services to the same customer. Cross-selling not only enhances customer convenience by providing a one-stop-shop for various financial needs but also creates synergies that drive revenue growth. For instance, a customer who holds a mortgage with the bank might also be interested in investment or insurance products. By identifying such opportunities, universal banks can deepen customer relationships and improve their overall financial health.

3) **Technology Adoption and Digital Transformation:**

The digital era has prompted universal banks to embrace technology in their operations. They develop innovative digital platforms, mobile applications, and online banking services to enhance customer experience, streamline processes, and improve accessibility to their services. Technology adoption also enables universal banks to offer personalized financial solutions, data-driven insights, and real-time updates, creating a more engaging and convenient banking experience for their customers.

4) **Corporate Governance and Ethical Conduct:**

Practices of universal banks emphasize strong corporate governance frameworks and ethical conduct. With their integrated model, universal banks face potential conflicts of interest between different business lines. Robust internal controls, transparent decision-making processes, and clear lines of accountability are essential to manage these conflicts and ensure that customer interests are protected. Ethical conduct is crucial in maintaining public trust and regulatory compliance, as well as upholding the integrity of the financial system.

5) **Regulatory Compliance and Risk Mitigation:**

Universal banks operate in a complex regulatory environment due to their involvement in diverse financial activities. Practices in this area focus on staying updated with evolving regulations, maintaining the necessary licenses, and implementing compliance procedures that align with industry standards. Risk mitigation strategies ensure that the institution adheres to regulatory requirements, minimizes legal and reputational risks, and contributes to the overall stability of the financial system.

6) **Innovation and Product Development:**

Innovation is a hallmark of universal banking practices. These institutions continuously seek to develop new financial products, services, and solutions that cater to evolving customer needs and market trends. Innovation helps universal banks remain competitive and relevant in a rapidly changing landscape, enabling them to offer cutting-edge solutions that address emerging challenges and opportunities.

7) **Community Engagement and Social Responsibility:**

Practices of universal banks extend beyond financial transactions to encompass community engagement and corporate social responsibility (CSR) initiatives. These banks recognize their role in promoting sustainable development and positive social impact. Through CSR initiatives, universal banks support educational programs, healthcare initiatives, environmental sustainability, and other projects that benefit the communities they serve, aligning their business activities with broader societal goals.

8) **Global Expansion and Cross-Border Operations:**

Many universal banks have a global presence and engage in cross-border operations. Practices in this context involve navigating complex international regulations, managing currency risks, and tailoring financial solutions to the unique needs of various markets. This global expansion allows universal banks to serve multinational corporations, facilitate international trade, and contribute to global economic growth.

9) **Client-Centric Approach and Relationship Building:**

Practices of universal banks emphasize a client-centric approach that prioritizes building strong and lasting relationships with customers. Universal banks offer personalized advisory services, financial planning, and wealth management solutions that cater to individual and business needs. This approach fosters customer loyalty, strengthens brand reputation, and positions universal banks as trusted financial partners.

10) **Employee Training and Skill Development:**

Given the diversity of financial services offered, universal banks invest in employee training and skill development. Staff members need to be well-versed in various financial products, regulatory requirements, and industry trends. Ongoing training ensures that employees can provide accurate information, deliver quality services, and maintain a high level of professionalism.

2.2 Advantages and Disadvantages of Universal Banking:

Universal banking offers several advantages, including economies of scale achieved through integrated operations, enhanced customer convenience due to a wide range of financial services under one roof, effective risk diversification across various business lines, and increased competitiveness through innovation and cross-selling. However, it also presents disadvantages such as potential conflicts of interest between different activities, regulatory complexities due to the need for comprehensive oversight, increased systemic risk as failures in one area could affect the entire institution, and challenges in maintaining expertise across diverse financial sectors, necessitating robust risk management and governance frameworks to harness the benefits while mitigating the potential drawbacks.

2.2.1 Advantages of Universal Banking:

Universal banking, characterized by its comprehensive range of financial services under one institutional umbrella, offers numerous advantages that contribute to its prominence in the modern financial landscape. Following are the Advantages of Universal Banking:

1) **Economies of Scale and Cost Efficiency**:
   Universal banking harnesses economies of scale by consolidating various financial services within a single entity. Shared resources, infrastructure, and operational efficiencies lead to reduced costs per unit of service, enhancing profitability. This cost advantage allows universal banks to offer competitive pricing to customers, ensuring affordability and accessibility to a wide range of financial products and services.
2) **Diverse Revenue Streams**:
   The integration of commercial banking, investment banking, insurance, and asset management diversifies revenue streams for universal banks. This diversity mitigates the impact of economic fluctuations on a single sector, ensuring stable income even when specific areas of the financial market experience downturns.
3) **Risk Diversification and Management**:
   Universal banks effectively manage risks through diversification across various financial activities. In adverse market conditions, potential losses in one sector can be offset by gains in others, enhancing overall financial stability. The ability to spread risk contributes to the resilience of universal banks and reduces their susceptibility to systemic shocks.
4) **Enhanced Customer Convenience and Cross-Selling Opportunities**:
   Universal banking simplifies customers' financial lives by offering a comprehensive suite of services in one place. Customers can access traditional banking services, investment opportunities, insurance products, and more, streamlining their financial management. Cross-selling opportunities arise as banks can offer tailored solutions to individual needs, deepening customer relationships and boosting revenue.

5) **Financial Inclusion and Access**:
Universal banks, with their extensive branch networks and digital platforms, promote financial inclusion by reaching underserved populations. They provide basic banking services, insurance, and investment opportunities to individuals and businesses in remote and rural areas, fostering economic growth and reducing inequality.

6) **Support for Businesses and Corporations**:
Universal banks cater to diverse financial needs of businesses, offering commercial banking services, investment banking solutions, trade finance, and advisory services. This comprehensive support fosters entrepreneurship, enables efficient capital allocation, and drives economic expansion.

7) **Innovation and Investment Opportunities**:
The integrated model encourages innovation as universal banks seek to develop new financial products and services to meet evolving market demands. They often pioneer novel financial instruments, investment vehicles, and technologies, spurring competition and technological advancement in the industry.

8) **Global Reach and International Transactions**:
Universal banks, with their multinational presence, facilitate cross-border transactions and international trade. They offer services such as forex operations, trade finance, and correspondent banking, contributing to global economic integration and financial connectivity.

9) **Efficient Allocation of Capital**:
Universal banks play a role in efficiently allocating capital by directing funds to sectors with promising growth prospects. They assist in channeling investments towards projects that drive economic development, job creation, and technological innovation.

10) **Financial Stability and Systemic Importance**:
Universal banks, due to their diversified operations, contribute to overall financial stability. Their ability to absorb shocks in one sector prevents cascading effects on the entire financial system, minimizing the likelihood of systemic crises.

11) **Support for Infrastructure and Development Projects**:
Universal banks often engage in project finance, funding large-scale infrastructure projects. Their involvement ensures that critical infrastructure developments, such as energy, transportation, and communication networks, receive necessary financial support.

12) **Holistic Financial Solutions**:
Universal banks provide holistic solutions that cater to various life stages and financial needs of customers. They offer retirement planning, investment advice, insurance coverage, and wealth management services, ensuring comprehensive financial planning for individuals and families.

13) Enhanced Competition and Innovation:

The presence of universal banks in the financial sector fosters healthy competition and spurs innovation. They introduce new financial products, technological advancements, and customer-centric services, compelling other institutions to adapt and innovate to remain relevant.

14) Maximized Resource Utilization:

Universal banks utilize their resources efficiently by pooling expertise from different financial sectors. This synergy enables them to address complex financial challenges, deliver sophisticated solutions, and respond adeptly to changing market dynamics.

15) Contribution to Economic Growth:

Universal banks contribute significantly to economic growth by supporting businesses, facilitating capital flow, promoting investment, and generating employment opportunities. Their multifaceted services stimulate economic activity and development.

16) Enhanced Access to Investment Banking Services:

Small and medium-sized enterprises (SMEs) often lack access to investment banking services. Universal banks bridge this gap by offering advisory services, capital raising, and access to financial markets, enabling SMEs to scale and innovate.

17) Effective Wealth Management:

High-net-worth individuals benefit from universal banks' wealth management services, which include portfolio diversification, tax planning, and estate management. These services optimize financial outcomes and provide tailored solutions for complex financial situations.

18) Strengthened Corporate Relationships:

Universal banks foster strong relationships with corporate clients by providing comprehensive financial services. This facilitates long-term collaboration, financial advisory and tailored solutions that address corporations' evolving financial needs.

19) Comprehensive Regulatory Frameworks:

Regulators often subject universal banks to comprehensive regulatory frameworks due to their integrated nature. This results in enhanced risk management practices, transparency, and accountability, contributing to a more stable and resilient financial system.

20) Strategic Alliances and Partnerships:

Universal banks can form strategic alliances with other institutions, leveraging their diverse capabilities to create mutually beneficial partnerships. These collaborations enhance innovation, expand market reach, and improve customer offerings.

2.2.2 Disadvantages of Universal Banking:

While universal banking offers a plethora of advantages, its integrated business model also presents several disadvantages that merit careful consideration. Following are the Disadvantages of Universal Banking:

1) **Conflicts of Interest**:
   One of the primary disadvantages of universal banking is the potential for conflicts of interest. When an institution engages in various financial activities under one roof, conflicts can arise between different business lines. For example, an investment banking division might be motivated to recommend financial products from other areas of the bank that generate higher fees, even if they are not the best fit for the customer's needs. These conflicts could compromise the objectivity and ethical conduct of the institution, undermining customer trust and the integrity of financial advice.

2) **Regulatory Complexities**:
   Universal banking operates within a complex regulatory landscape due to its involvement in diverse financial sectors. Regulatory requirements vary for different activities, leading to challenges in maintaining compliance across all areas. Regulators must strike a balance between ensuring comprehensive oversight and avoiding overregulation that could stifle innovation. Universal banks must navigate intricate regulatory frameworks, allocate resources for compliance, and remain vigilant to changes in regulations across multiple jurisdictions.

3) **Systemic Risk**:
   The integrated nature of universal banks can lead to increased systemic risk. If a significant event occurs in one sector, it could have cascading effects on other areas of the institution, potentially destabilizing the entire financial system. The collapse of a large universal bank could have far-reaching consequences, affecting both traditional banking and investment banking activities, and causing disruptions to markets, customers, and counterparties.

4) **Expertise and Skill Maintenance**:
   Maintaining expertise across diverse financial sectors poses a challenge for universal banks. Different sectors require distinct skill sets, and ensuring that employees are well-versed in all areas is demanding. This challenge extends to recruiting, training, and retaining talent with expertise in commercial banking, investment banking, insurance, and asset management. Failure to maintain high levels of expertise could lead to suboptimal decision-making, diminished customer satisfaction, and increased exposure to risks.

5) **Corporate Governance Concerns**:
   Universal banks face corporate governance challenges due to their integrated model. Managing conflicts of interest, aligning business practices with ethical

guidelines, and ensuring accountability across various business lines can be complex. Effective corporate governance becomes critical to prevent undue concentration of power, maintain transparency, and uphold the best interests of shareholders, customers, and the wider financial system.

6) **Operational Complexity**:

The breadth of services offered by universal banks results in operational complexity. Coordinating operations across multiple business lines, managing diverse technology systems, and integrating different organizational structures can be challenging. This complexity might hinder agility and responsiveness, making it difficult for universal banks to adapt swiftly to changing market conditions or seize emerging opportunities.

7) **Size and Systemic Importance**:

Large universal banks can become "too big to fail," posing systemic risks if they encounter financial distress. Governments and regulators might feel compelled to bail out these institutions to prevent cascading effects on the broader economy. This phenomenon undermines market discipline, moral hazard, and fairness, as smaller institutions do not receive the same level of support.

8) **Limited Specialization**:

Universal banks might spread their resources and expertise thin across various financial services, leading to limited specialization in any single area. This could result in reduced competitiveness in comparison to specialized institutions that focus exclusively on one sector. Customers seeking specialized services might opt for niche players rather than universal banks.

9) **Regulatory Capture**:

The extensive operations of universal banks might grant them undue influence over regulatory bodies. This could lead to regulatory capture, where institutions use their size and influence to shape regulations to their advantage. This situation undermines fair competition, erodes trust in the financial system, and might lead to regulatory measures that favor larger players over smaller competitors.

10) **Lack of Customer-Centric Focus**:

The sheer scope of universal banking operations might dilute their customer-centric focus. While customers benefit from comprehensive offerings, the personalized attention and specialized services they receive from smaller, niche institutions could be compromised. Universal banks might struggle to provide the same level of attention and tailored solutions that specialized entities can deliver.

11) **Risk Concentration**:

While universal banks diversify risks across various sectors, they could unintentionally concentrate risks in certain sectors due to market trends or investment strategies. For instance, a universal bank heavily invested in a specific sector that experiences a downturn might face significant losses that offset gains in other areas.

12) **Lack of Innovation in Certain Sectors**:

Universal banks might prioritize innovation in more profitable sectors while neglecting innovation in less lucrative areas. This imbalance could hinder the development of innovative solutions in sectors such as traditional banking services, leading to missed opportunities for improving customer experience and operational efficiency.

13) **Market Distortions**:

Universal banks' significant market presence might distort competition in certain sectors. Smaller, specialized institutions might struggle to compete against universal banks' vast resources and service offerings. This could limit the diversity of financial service providers and reduce customer choice.

14) **Complicated Organizational Structure**:

The integration of various financial services within a universal bank can lead to a complicated organizational structure. Multiple divisions, business units, and product lines might result in bureaucracy, communication challenges, and decision-making bottlenecks that hinder agility and responsiveness.

15) **Inefficient Resource Allocation**:

Universal banks might allocate resources inefficiently across different business lines, favoring more profitable areas at the expense of others. This allocation might not align with customer needs or market demands, resulting in suboptimal resource utilization and missed growth opportunities.

2.3 Problem Faced by Universal Banks:

Universal banks, with their integrated model offering a wide range of financial services, encounter various challenges that can impact their operations, customer relationships, regulatory compliance, and overall business performance. These challenges reflect the complexities inherent in managing diverse financial activities under one institutional umbrella. Here are some of the key problems faced by universal banks:

1) **Conflicts of Interest**:

Universal banks often face conflicts of interest due to their involvement in different financial sectors. Balancing the interests of clients across various services while maintaining ethical conduct can be challenging. For instance, an investment banking division might recommend products from other divisions of the bank that generate higher fees, even if they are not the best fit for the customer's needs. This can erode customer trust and undermine the integrity of financial advice.

2) **Regulatory Complexity**:

Universal banks operate in a complex regulatory environment due to their involvement in diverse financial activities. Compliance with different regulatory frameworks, reporting requirements, and risk management standards can be daunting. Adapting to changing regulations and ensuring consistent compliance across all sectors poses a significant challenge that requires dedicated resources and expertise.

3) **Risk Management**:

   Managing risks effectively across various business lines can be intricate. Universal banks need to identify, assess, and mitigate risks associated with different financial services, including credit risk, market risk, operational risk, and regulatory risk. Ensuring a comprehensive risk management approach that considers the interconnectedness of different activities is essential to maintain stability.

4) **Operational Complexity**:

   The integration of multiple financial services can lead to operational complexity. Coordinating processes, technology systems, and personnel across different business lines requires efficient management. Operational inefficiencies can hinder agility, responsiveness, and customer service, impacting the overall customer experience.

5) **Corporate Governance Challenges**:

   The integrated nature of universal banking poses challenges for corporate governance. Ensuring transparency, accountability, and ethical behavior across diverse business lines can be demanding. Managing conflicts of interest, avoiding undue concentration of power, and maintaining the trust of stakeholders are crucial components of effective corporate governance.

6) **Systemic Risk**:

   Due to their size and interconnectedness, large universal banks can pose systemic risks to the financial system. If a major universal bank encounters financial distress, it could trigger cascading effects that destabilize the entire economy. Regulators need to strike a balance between promoting competition and mitigating systemic risks associated with universal banks.

7) **Expertise and Skill Maintenance**:

   Maintaining expertise across various financial sectors is challenging. Universal banks require a workforce that is well-versed in commercial banking, investment banking, insurance, and asset management. Recruiting, training, and retaining talent with diverse skill sets can be difficult, potentially leading to suboptimal decision-making and customer service.

8) **Customer-Centric Focus**:

   The breadth of services offered by universal banks can dilute their customer-centric focus. Ensuring personalized attention, tailored solutions, and specialized expertise in each service area becomes more challenging as the range of services expands. Some customers may prefer the specialized expertise of niche institutions.

9) **Technological Integration**:
Universal banks need to integrate technology across various business lines to provide seamless customer experiences. Coordinating different technological systems, platforms, and digital services can be complex and require significant investment in IT infrastructure.

10) **Market Distortions**:
Universal banks' market dominance can distort competition in certain sectors. Smaller, specialized institutions may struggle to compete against universal banks' vast resources and service offerings. This can limit the diversity of financial service providers and reduce customer choice.

11) **Regulatory Capture**:
Universal banks' size and influence might lead to regulatory capture, where institutions shape regulations to their advantage. This can undermine fair competition, impede innovation, and lead to regulatory measures that favor larger players.

12) **Size and Systemic Importance**:
The size of universal banks can lead to the perception that they are "too big to fail." This can create moral hazard, as governments and regulators may feel compelled to bail out these institutions to prevent economic instability, which undermines market discipline.

13) **Efficient Resource Allocation**:
Universal banks might allocate resources inefficiently across different business lines, favoring more profitable areas over others. This could result in suboptimal allocation of resources that do not align with customer needs or market demands.

2.4 Recent Trends in Universal Banking in India:

Recent trends in universal banking in India reflect the dynamic evolution of the financial sector, driven by technological advancements, regulatory changes, customer preferences, and global economic shifts. Universal banks, which offer a wide range of financial services under one institutional umbrella, have adapted to these trends to enhance customer experiences, improve operational efficiency, manage risks, and stay competitive. Following are the recent trends in universal banking in India:

1) **Digital Transformation and Fintech Integration:**
Universal banks in India have embraced digital transformation as a key trend. Rapid technology adoption, driven by changing customer expectations, has led to the development of robust digital platforms, mobile banking apps, and online services. The integration of fintech solutions, such as digital payments, robo-advisory, and blockchain technology, has enhanced customer convenience, enabled efficient transactions, and improved access to financial services, especially in remote and underserved areas.

2) **Personalization and Customer-Centric Approach:**
Recent trends emphasize a customer-centric approach in universal banking. Banks leverage data analytics and AI-driven insights to understand individual customer preferences and behaviors. This data-driven approach enables banks to offer personalized financial solutions, tailored advice, and targeted product offerings, enhancing customer engagement and loyalty.

3) **Open Banking and Collaboration:**
Open banking initiatives are gaining traction in India, fostering collaboration between universal banks and fintech firms. APIs (Application Programming Interfaces) allow third-party developers to access bank data securely and develop innovative financial products and services. This trend promotes innovation, expands service offerings, and creates a more competitive landscape.

4) **Wealth Management and Investment Advisory Services:**
Universal banks are increasingly focusing on providing comprehensive wealth management and investment advisory services. As customers seek guidance for optimizing their financial portfolios, banks offer sophisticated investment strategies, portfolio diversification, and retirement planning solutions to cater to diverse wealth management needs.

5) **Regulatory Changes and Governance Enhancements:**
Recent regulatory changes in India have impacted universal banking operations. Regulatory authorities are strengthening governance frameworks, enhancing transparency, and introducing measures to manage conflicts of interest within integrated institutions. Universal banks are adapting to these changes by improving internal controls, ethical conduct, and risk management practices.

6) **Risk Management and Compliance:**
Universal banks are investing in advanced risk management technologies and methodologies to navigate an evolving risk landscape. The integration of various financial activities requires banks to adopt sophisticated risk assessment models, stress testing, and scenario analysis to ensure effective risk management across all sectors.

7) **Sustainable Banking and ESG Integration:**
Environmental, Social, and Governance (ESG) considerations have gained prominence in recent years. Universal banks are aligning their operations with sustainable practices, offering ESG-compliant financial products and integrating responsible investment strategies. This trend reflects a growing awareness of the social and environmental impact of financial activities.

8) **Innovation in Payments and Financial Inclusion:**
Universal banks are driving innovation in payment systems to cater to the digital payment revolution in India. They are collaborating with payment aggregators, fintech firms, and government initiatives to offer seamless and secure digital

payment solutions that cater to diverse customer needs while promoting financial inclusion.

9) **Focus on Cybersecurity and Data Privacy:**
As digital banking gains prominence, universal banks are ramping up cybersecurity measures to protect customer data and financial transactions. Trends include adopting advanced encryption techniques, biometric authentication, and AI-based fraud detection systems to ensure the integrity of digital banking operations.

10) **Expansion of Digital Lending:**
Digital lending platforms have emerged as a significant trend in universal banking. These platforms leverage technology to assess creditworthiness quickly and offer instant loans to individuals and businesses. This trend enhances financial access, streamlines loan processing, and reduces the burden of paperwork.

11) **Remote Banking and Video KYC:**
The COVID-19 pandemic accelerated the adoption of remote banking services and video-based Know Your Customer (KYC) processes. Universal banks integrated video KYC to onboard customers remotely, ensuring compliance with regulatory norms while offering a safe and efficient customer onboarding experience.

12) **Focus on Micro, Small, and Medium Enterprises (MSMEs):**
Universal banks are increasingly focusing on serving the MSME sector, which plays a crucial role in India's economy. Tailored financial products, digital lending solutions, trade finance, and business advisory services are being offered to support MSME growth, boost entrepreneurship, and drive economic development.

13) **Enhanced Corporate Governance and Ethics:**
Universal banks are placing greater emphasis on corporate governance and ethical conduct to address potential conflicts of interest arising from their integrated model. They are enhancing internal controls, introducing clear accountability structures, and implementing risk committees to ensure transparency and ethical behavior.

14) **Global Expansion and Cross-Border Operations:**
Some Indian universal banks are exploring global expansion through cross-border operations, aiming to tap into international markets and cater to the needs of multinational corporations. This trend enables banks to offer comprehensive solutions to businesses engaged in cross-border trade and investments.

15) **Robust Customer Data Protection:**
Given the increasing digitization of banking operations, universal banks are investing in robust customer data protection measures. They are adopting encryption, secure cloud storage, and data access controls to safeguard sensitive customer information from cyber threats and unauthorized access.

16) **Compliance with International Standards:**
As India aligns with international financial standards, universal banks are adopting practices that align with global best practices in risk management, customer

protection, anti-money laundering (AML), and counter-terrorism financing (CTF) measures. This alignment enhances India's standing in the global financial landscape.

17) **Focus on Financial Education and Literacy:**
Universal banks are placing emphasis on financial education and literacy initiatives. They are launching programs to enhance customers' understanding of financial products, investments, and money management, contributing to improved financial decision-making.

****

Multiple Choice Questions

1) **Universal banks follow ________________ practices by integrating a range of financial services under a single institution.**
   a) Financial management
   b) universal banking
   c) Cultural integration
   d) Linguistic diversity
2) **One common practice is ________________, where customers can access various financial products and services through a single point.**
   a) quality control
   b) financial convenience
   c) inventory management
   d) artistic expressions
3) **Universal banks may offer ________________ accounts to cater to different customer segments and financial needs.**
   a) Financial analysis
   b) customized
   c) Supply chain management
   d) Linguistic diversity
4) **The practice of ________________ involves cross-selling products like loans, insurance, and investments to existing customers.**
   a) quality control
   b) cross-marketing
   c) financial analysis
   d) cultural integration
5) **________________ is a strategy where universal banks collaborate with fintech companies to enhance their digital offerings.**
   a) inventory management
   b) fintech integration
   c) linguistic diversity
   d) quality control
6) **Universal banks also engage in ________________ by providing advisory and consultancy services to clients.**
   a) cultural integration
   b) financial advisory
   c) linguistic diversity
   d) inventory management
7) **One ________________ of universal banking is the ability to offer diverse financial services, catering to various customer needs.**

a) Financial management b) advantage
c) Cultural integration d) Linguistic diversity

8) Universal banks can achieve ______________ by cross-selling products to existing customers, increasing revenue streams.

a) quality control b) economies of scope
c) inventory management d) artistic expressions

9) The integration of various financial services can lead to ______________ customer relationships and loyalty.

a) Financial analysis b) strengthened
c) Supply chain management d) Linguistic diversity

10) However, one ______________ of universal banking is the potential for conflicts of interest due to the wide range of services.

a) quality control b) disadvantage
c) financial analysis d) cultural integration

11) Universal banks can benefit from ______________ diversification, reducing risks associated with fluctuations in individual markets.

a) inventory management b) risk
c) linguistic diversity d) quality control

12) A ______________ of universal banking is the complexity in managing diverse operations and regulatory challenges.

a) cultural integration b) disadvantage
c) linguistic diversity d) inventory management

13) Universal banks often face challenges in managing ______________ between different business segments, potentially leading to conflicts of interest.

a) Financial management b) synergies
c) Cultural integration d) Linguistic diversity

14) Regulatory ______________ can arise due to the diverse range of financial services offered by universal banks.

a) quality control b) compliance
c) inventory management d) artistic expressions

15) Maintaining a ______________ organizational structure can be complex and require effective coordination among various units.

a) Financial analysis b) diversified
c) Supply chain management d) Linguistic diversity

16) One challenge is managing ______________ risks associated with different financial activities and markets.

a) quality control b) risk diversification
c) financial analysis d) cultural integration

17) Ensuring effective ________________ and avoiding conflicts of interest can be difficult in universal banking.

a) inventory management
b) risk management
c) linguistic diversity
d) quality control

18) Universal banks may face difficulty in delivering ________________ customer experiences due to the complexity of their operations.

a) cultural integration
b) seamless
c) linguistic diversity
d) inventory management

19) ________________ have gained traction in India's banking sector, allowing customers to access various services through digital platforms.

a) Digital banking solutions
b) Branch expansion
c) Cultural integration
d) Asset management

20) Banks in India have been focusing on ________________ by offering integrated financial solutions to cater to a wider range of customer needs.

a) quality control
b) diversification
c) inventory management
d) artistic expressions

21) With the rise of fintech, there has been an emphasis on ________________ partnerships between traditional banks and technology startups.

a) Financial analysis
b) collaboration
c) Supply chain management
d) Linguistic diversity

22) ________________ have played a significant role in enhancing customer experience, providing personalized services, and efficient transactions.

a) Customer relationship management systems
b) Inventory management
c) Linguistic diversity
d) Quality control

23) Universal banks in India have been adapting to the ________________ by offering seamless online services and contactless transactions.

a) digital era
b) cultural integration
c) inventory optimization
d) financial analysis

24) Regulatory developments and ________________ have been influencing the strategies and operations of universal banks in India.

a) compliance requirements
b) linguistic diversity
c) financial management
d) asset management

Ans : **1)** b, **2)** b, **3)** b, **4)** b, **5)** b, **6)** b, **7)** b, **8)** b, **9)** b, **10)** b, **11)** b, **12)** b, **13)** b, **14)** b, **15)** b, **16)** b, **17)** b, **18)** b, **19)** a, **20)** b, **21)** b, **22)** a, **23)** a, **24)** a.

★★★★★★★

Review Questions

Q.1. Explain in detail the Practices of Universal Banks.

Q.2. State the Advantages of Universal Banking.

Q.3. Explain the Disadvantages of Universal Banking.

Q.4. Explain in detail about the Problem Faced by the Universal Banks.

Q.5. Explain about the Recent Trends in Universal Banks in India.

Q.6. **Write Short Notes on Following:**

a) Practices of Universal Banks
b) Advantages of Universal Banks
c) Disadvantages of Universal Banks

****

NOTES